Foundations for Life

Bible Studies From the Editors of *Decision* Magazine

Compiled and Edited by
Dr. Penelope J. Stokes

World Wide Publications
A Ministry of the Billy Graham Evangelistic Association
1303 Hennepin Ave., Minneapolis, MN 55403

Foundations for Life
© 1988 Billy Graham Evangelistic Association.

All rights reserved. No part of this publication may be reproduced in any form without written permission from the publisher: World Wide Publications, 1303 Hennepin Avenue, Minneapolis, Minnesota 55403.

World Wide Publications is the publishing ministry of the Billy Graham Evangelistic Association.

Scripture quotations, unless otherwise marked, are taken from The Holy Bible, New International Version, copyright © 1973, 1978, 1984, International Bible Society. Used by permission of Zondervan Bible Publishers.

Scripture quotations marked KJV are taken from the King James Version.

Scripture quotations marked NKJV are taken by permission from The New King James Version, copyright © 1979, 1980, 1982 Thomas Nelson, Inc., Thomas Nelson Publishers.

Scripture quotations marked RSV are taken by permission from the Revised Standard Version Bible, copyright © 1946, 1952, 1971, 1973 National Council of Churches of Christ in the U.S.A., New York, New York.

Scripture quotations marked NASB are taken by permission from the New American Standard Bible, © 1960, 1962, 1963, 1968, 1971, 1972, 1973, 1975, 1977 The Lockman Foundation, La Habra, California.

Scripture quotations marked NEB are taken by permission from the New English Bible. Copyright © the Delegates of the Oxford University Press and the Syndics of the Cambridge University Press, 1961, 1970.

Bible study lessons are taken by permission from Decision magazine, October 1985, October 1986, July/August 1986, September 1984, June 1986, June 1984. Copyright © 1984, 1985, 1986, the Billy Graham Evangelistic Association.

ISBN 0-89066-125-1

Printed in the United States of America

Contents

Introduction 1

Lessons 1 and 2:
Forgiveness *by John F. Walvoord* 2

Lessons 3 and 4:
Reconciliation *by Douglas Stuart* 10

Lessons 5 and 6:
Repentance *by James F. Breckenridge* 18

Lessons 7 and 8:
Fellowship *by Lewis Foster* 26

Lessons 9 and 10:
Mercy *by Richard B. Gaffin, Jr.* 34

Lessons 11 and 12:
Love *by J. Gordon Harris* 42

Notes 50

About the Authors 51

Introduction

It has happened! And we are delighted. For several years *Decision* magazine has been publishing a significant Bible study selection in each issue, written by outstanding Bible scholars, with practical application to our lives. The response to these Bible studies has been outstanding. Readers are telling the *Decision* editors, "I like this."

"This has helped me."

"I am growing."

The many such positive reactions over the years made it easy for us to decide, "Let's bring these Bible studies together in book form."

You now hold in your hand *Foundations for Life,* one of the first four collections of *Decision* Bible studies.

You will see right away that *Foundations for Life* is thoroughly biblical, with ample Scripture references to help you glean God's solid truth.

The studies are also practical. They will help you grow. You will stretch and mature in the faith whether you are enjoying the studies on your own, or with your Bible study class at church, or with a study group in your home.

The questions that go along with each study will help you, too. Ask them of yourself. Ask them of your group. Discuss them with others and you will all benefit.

There are twelve lessons in each book, making these studies ideal for Sunday school curriculum. It is equivalent to a full quarter of study in your church class.

If you like the material in *Foundations for Life*—and we think you will—see the back cover for a listing of the other three volumes of *Decision* Bible studies. When you have all four, you will have a complete year's Bible study on a variety of topics and themes, written by some of the keenest minds in the Christian world.

It is rewarding to understand God's Word better. It is exciting to have passages open up with clarity. It is good when, with wonder and awe, we can say to God, "Now I love your Word even more."

Roger C. Palms, Editor
Decision Magazine

Lesson 1
Forgiveness—God's Part

Seeking Forgiveness

"I marvel at God's infinite patience with me. When I do wrong, he could so easily turn away, but instead, when I seek forgiveness, he never fails to give it. Such love is truly divine."

—*Aileen Williams*[1]

If we claim to be without sin, we deceive ourselves and the truth is not in us. (1 John 1:8)

The first step in finding forgiveness is facing our need for forgiveness. Whether we are aware of it or not, deep in the soul of every person is the thirst to be forgiven, the desire to have a right relationship with God. In many cases this desire is buried, covered beneath years of stifling any thought of seeking God. Ignorance of God and his salvation, repeated sin against conscience, and the desire to justify ourselves hinder our efforts to find forgiveness. In folk religions the desire for forgiveness and the fear of the "unknown God" prompt all kinds of religious acts of sacrifice to idols and evil spirits. Yet this process ends with the burden of guilt and fear increased. Except for Christian faith, no religion offers a sure experience of forgiveness.

Facing our guilt and sin honestly is the first step; then we must seek forgiveness. Judas Iscariot said to the priest, "I have sinned . . . for I have betrayed innocent blood" (Matthew 27:4). Judas had heard many messages from Jesus, had enjoyed being in the inner circle of the twelve disciples, and had seen Jesus perform miracles. But the promised kingdom and the hope of wealth and prominence that Judas wanted were not being realized. Having only a superficial faith, he was not prepared to accept the cross. After Judas betrayed Jesus, his remorse and confession of sin were not enough to secure forgiveness. His double life of hypocrisy and pretended religion had led to total moral collapse. He had faced the reality of guilt but had not sought forgiveness.

—*John F. Walvoord*

For Personal Insight and Group Discussion

1. Give a brief practical definition of "sin." What does the Bible say about the universality of sin? (See Isaiah 64:6; Romans 3:9-17,23.)

2. In John 16:7-11, Jesus says that the Holy Spirit convicts a person of sin. In what specific ways do I become aware of the Spirit's conviction in my life?

3. Consider 2 Samuel 12:1-13; 2 Samuel 24:10; and Nehemiah 1:6,7. What do the confessions of David and Nehemiah demonstrate about honest confession?

4. Why do I resist confessing my sin? What assurance does Deuteronomy 4:29 give about God's readiness to forgive?

5. What are some of the results I see when I realize the forgiveness of my sins?

Finding Forgiveness

"When God forgives a man, he not only alters him but transmutes what he has already done. Forgiveness does not mean merely that I am saved from sin and made right for heaven; forgiveness means that I am forgiven into a recreated relationship to God."

—*Oswald Chambers*[2]

If we confess our sins, he is faithful and just and will forgive us our sins and purify us from all unrighteousness. (1 John 1:9)

This promise is addressed to John's "dear children" (1 John 2:1); forgiveness is offered to those who already belong to Christ. But what about non-Christians?

On the day of Pentecost the people "said to Peter and the other apostles, 'Brothers, what shall we do?'" (Acts 2:37). Peter answered, "Repent and be baptized, every one of you, in the name of Jesus Christ so that your sins may be forgiven. And you will receive the gift of the Holy Spirit" (v. 38). The word "repent" is often interpreted to mean "sorrow for sin"; but sorrow for sin does not save, as the case of Judas demonstrates. The word "repent" actually means "change your mind." The people in Acts 2 had rejected the teaching that Jesus was the Son of God. Peter calls on them to change their minds, to exercise faith in Christ—an act of the will deciding to receive Christ. There must be a deliberate act of trusting in Christ as the One who died for our sins and rose again. (See 1 Corinthians 15:1-4.) This act of faith involves the whole person—the will, the mind, and the emotions. Essentially repentance is a decision of the will based on some comprehension of the truth of the gospel. It may be accompanied to some extent by emotions, but it is a choice, a decision.

Christians are forgiven when they are saved. 1 John 1:9 refers to our experience of forgiveness. As we become conscious of sins in our Christian lives, we experience a sense of estrangement from God which can be resolved only by confession, which makes the life of fellowship possible. John refers to this fellowship when he writes, "If we walk in the light, as he is in the light, we have fellowship with one another, and the blood of Jesus, his Son, purifies us from every sin" (1 John 1:7). This daily experience of forgiveness is the secret of inner peace. God is ready to forgive, yet to experience that forgiveness we must be walking in fellowship with him. Honest confession of sin is the key to experiencing forgiveness.

—John F. Walvoord

For Personal Insight and Group Discussion

1. In Isaiah 1:18, God initiates forgiveness with the words, "Come now, let us reason together." In what ways is repentance a reasonable choice to make?

2. What is God's perspective on forgiven sin? (Psalm 103:12; Isaiah 43:25) Why do I often continue to carry the burden of guilt over sin that has been forgiven and "cast away"?

3. The person who has been forgiven is called "blessed" or "happy" (Psalm 32:1,2; Romans 4:7,8). How do I respond to the experience of having my sins forgiven?

4. According to Hebrews 9:22, why was the death of Christ necessary for my forgiveness?

5. How would my life and attitudes change if I consistently lived in an awareness of God's forgiveness?

Lesson 2
Forgiveness—Our Part

Forgiving Others

"The Bible commands us to put bitterness away; we are to forgive others whether or not they solicit our forgiveness. Yet many Christians believe that they can't forgive until they feel like it! They think that if they forgive when they don't feel like it, they are hypocritical.

You know that you cannot switch your emotions on and off. You cannot develop the right feelings on your own. But God is not mocking you when he tells you to forgive; you can choose to do so, whether or not you feel like it. "

—*Erwin W. Lutzer*[3]

Be kind and compassionate to one another, forgiving each other, just as in Christ God forgave you. (Ephesians 4:32)

A Christian seeking forgiveness from God will not find the real experience of forgiveness unless he in turn forgives those who have sinned against him. In Matthew 18, Peter asked, "Lord, how many times shall I forgive my brother when he sins against me? Up to seven times?"

The Lord replied, "I tell you, not seven times but seventy-seven times" (Matthew 18:21,22).

Jesus went on to drive his point home with an illustration: a servant who had been forgiven a debt of 10,000 talents then cast his fellow servant into prison for a small debt. A Christian, having received mercy and forgiveness from God, should extend mercy and forgiveness to others. Such forgiveness is not only necessary for enjoyment of close fellowship with God, but is necessary for our own inner peace as well. One who hates others and is constantly bringing up their sins and acts of unkindness hurts himself more than anyone else. We should not only forgive, but we must also forget.

Salvation is an undeserved gift and is not canceled when we fail to measure up to God's high standards of spiritual life. But we will never truly feel forgiven until we learn to forgive others. It is impossible to walk in fellowship with God unless our own heart is right toward God and toward others.

—John F. Walvoord

For Personal Insight and Group Discussion

1. In the Lord's Prayer, Jesus taught his disciples to pray, "Forgive us our sins as we forgive those who sin against us." Why is forgiveness of others a vital factor in my own experience of God's forgiveness?

2. Have I ever held a grudge or harbored bitterness and unforgiveness against another person? What was the result of that unforgiveness in terms of the relationship? Within myself?

3. Have I ever freely forgiven someone who has wronged me before he or she asked for forgiveness? What was the result—within me, or in the relationship—of that forgiveness?

4. How does unforgiveness interfere with my fellowship with God? (See 1 John 4:20.)

5. How can I forgive as "an act of the will" when I don't feel like forgiving? What can I do to help my emotions come into line with my action of obedience?

Beyond Forgiveness

"There is an art of forgetting, and every Christian should become skilled in it. Forgetting the things which are behind is a positive necessity if we are to become more than mere babes in Christ. If we cannot trust God to have dealt effectively with our past, we may as well throw in the sponge now and have it over with. Fifty years of grieving over our sins cannot blot out their guilt. But if God has indeed pardoned and cleansed us, then we should count it done and waste no more time in sterile lamentations."

—A.W. Tozer[4]

Therefore, since we have been justified through faith, we have peace with God through our Lord Jesus Christ, through whom we have gained access by faith into this grace in which we now stand. And we rejoice in the hope of the glory of God. (Romans 5:1,2)

When Christ died on the cross for our sins, he not only provided a just basis for God to forgive our sins, but he also made possible a new standing of grace with God based on God's declaration that those who believe in him have his righteousness.

How wonderful to know that all our sins are forgiven because they were nailed to the cross almost 2,000 years ago! Colossians 2:13,14 says, "He [God] forgave us all our sins, having canceled the written code, . . . nailing it to the cross." Christ's death met the full demands of the law.

But a Christian has more than forgiveness, the negation of condemning sin. He has justification. Being justified means that God has not only forgiven us, but has declared us righteous. Because we are in Christ, God sees us in the perfection of the Person and work of his Son. Our standing with God is as righteous as Christ himself. Our present spiritual state falls far short of this perfection, but in heaven our spiritual state will be raised to the high level of the justification which we now have in Christ.

If one overdraws his checking account and the bank nevertheless honors his check, that person has a debt to the bank. He will be forgiven if he pays what is due. But if a friend should deposit a large sum of money to his account, it will not only wipe out the debt but will give him a large balance. This is the situation with the Christian. We are not only forgiven, we are justified and declared righteous by a righteous God who sees us in the perfection of his Son. What we cannot earn, deserve, or buy, God gives us freely when we believe in Christ.

—John F. Walvoord

For Personal Insight and Group Discussion

1. What does "justification" mean? Why does God declare me justified in Christ?

2. Are there times when I don't feel justified? Why, when God has forgiven me, do I sometimes find it difficult to forgive myself?

3. Are there sins in my life that I have been reluctant to surrender to Christ? How can I take steps to repent of them and receive forgiveness? (See 1 John 1:8,9.)

4. Are there individuals who have wronged me against whom I still harbor unforgiveness and bitterness? What steps can I take to clear the slate where those relationships are concerned?

5. If I believe that   a) I am a sinner,   b) God has forgiven my sins, and   c) I am justified in his sight, how will that belief affect my conduct and attitudes?

Lesson 3
Reconciliation—With Our Father

Ready and Waiting

"Man's wrenching desire to find inner peace accounts for the faddish popularity of the consciousness movement. But that only makes matters worse, because disillusionment sets in when we succeed in learning who we really are.

There is only one way out of the agonizing dilemma. It is not through ourselves, but through the One who took your sins and mine upon himself on the cross.

The corollary to man's repentance is God's grace, his loving forgiveness. . . . only through the power of Christ's resurrection can we find the forgiveness which makes life bearable."

—*Charles Colson*[5]

In Christ God was reconciling the world to himself, not counting their trespasses against them, and entrusting to us the message of reconciliation. (2 Corinthians 5:19, RSV)

The word "reconciliation" means making friends of former enemies, or putting on good terms again people separated by rejection. For estranged persons to be reconciled, they have to be willing to put the past behind them, make up, and be friends again. Of course, they need not have harmed each other equally. One might have a lot more forgiving to do than the other!

Our separation from God as a result of our sin is the most dangerous, unreconciled condition any human being can be in. It goes far beyond the alienation of one person from another. The Bible is consistent in the way it speaks of reconciliation with God: we don't do it, God does. God was never at fault. We don't need to bring him back to a faithful, loving relationship. Rather, we are the ones who need to be reconciled.

God has already accomplished our reconciliation to him through the work of Christ on the cross. Because Christ died for the whole world, we all have the potential to have our trespasses forgiven. But people must believe and act on the "message," the gospel of reconciliation.

For many reasons—hatred, habit, stubbornness, selfishness—people resist hearing God's wonderful message of reconciliation. But the message is true; God waits for acceptance of his promise: "In Christ God was reconciling the world to himself" (2 Corinthians 5:19,RSV).

—Douglas Stuart

For Personal Insight and Group Discussion

1. Why do I need to be "reconciled" to God? (See Isaiah 59:2.)

2. Is reconciliation a one-time experience or an ongoing process? How do I know? (See Romans 5:1-5.)

3. What are the results of not being reconciled to God?

4. What benefits do I experience from being reconciled to him?

Kingdom and Family

"Reconciliation brings love where there was hate, acceptance where there was rejection, fellowship where there was estrangement."

—*Jeri Sweany*[6]

So then you are no longer strangers and sojourners, but you are fellow citizens with the saints and members of the household of God. (Ephesians 2:19,20, RSV)

A "stranger," in the sense that Paul uses the word here, is not merely an outsider, who may someday be accepted as a citizen, but someone who doesn't by right belong in a place and cannot expect to stay there forever. "Sojourners" are not citizens of a given place and thus do not legally "belong" there, but they are allowed to pass through or to stay for a while.

When Abraham lived in Canaan, he was "a stranger and a sojourner" (Genesis 23:4,RSV). Even though he was allowed to buy property and to bury his wife, he was not a citizen. So it was with the Israelites in Egypt. They were in places where they did not belong.

Paul calls us spiritual sojourners; we once did not belong, but now this is no longer the case. We were outsiders, strangers and sojourners, not yet belonging to God's kingdom and family.

But no one can force his way into the kingdom. No one can demand to belong. Citizenship in God's kingdom is based on reconciliation to God. Membership in God's family (household) cannot be obtained by any means other than that established by the head of the family. The Bible talks both about our being born into God's family and also about being adopted into it (John 1:12,13; Galatians 4:5). It is the will of the Father that makes the new membership possible. It is his will to invite everyone to come, so that no one need remain a stranger, outside the family, unreconciled.

Our fellow citizens in the kingdom, our fellow family members, are those who are reconciled and are made holy by God. We enjoy our fellowship in God's family because God has accepted us.

—Douglas Stuart

For Personal Insight and Group Discussion

1. The Bible indicates that, while we once were strangers to the kingdom of God, we now are strangers and sojourners in this world. We live here, but we have our citizenship and belonging in another kingdom. What kinds of problems arise from this duality? (See 1 Peter 2:10,11; 4:3,4.)

2. How do I become a member of God's household?

3. What is it like to be a stranger, an outsider? Have I ever felt like an outsider in the body of Christ?

4. Whom does God invite to become members of his family? (See John 3:16.) Are there times I have shunned those he has invited, making them feel like outsiders?

5. What, specifically, have I or others done to exclude another person from fellowship? What can I do to make others feel welcome, invited, accepted into fellowship with Christ and his body?

Lesson 4
Reconciliation With the Family

Like Loving Brothers

"When Christians in a local church understand and practice right attitudes in their relations with each other, the most solid foundation for unity has been laid. Then believers can forget themselves, and serve each other, bound together by the practical loving that undertakes to meet the needs of the individual."

—*Marion Leach Jacobsen*[7]

Esau ran to meet Jacob and embraced him; he threw his arms around his neck and kissed him. And they wept. (Genesis 33:4)

The Bible's primary emphasis is the reconciliation of men and women to God. But there is also a concern that we who are God's children should be reconciled to one another—that those who claim to know God through his Son Jesus Christ should act like brothers and sisters.

Jesus said, "All men will know that you are my disciples if you love one another" (John 13:35). A natural result of our reconciliation to God ought to be reconciliation to each other, so that no enmity remains among us. The story of Esau and Jacob helps remind us that even bitter divisions can be overcome if there is a will to do so.

Jacob did not hesitate to use questionable means to advance himself. Perhaps his most outrageous display of self-advancement occurred when he deceived his father and manipulated his brother in order to receive the coveted blessing of the eldest son (Genesis 27:1-40). And Esau was hardly guiltless in this arrangement, since he had sold his birthright blessing for a good meal—a sign that he did not take his father's relationship with God seriously.

Eventually, Jacob and Esau became enemies, and Esau determined to kill his brother (v. 41). Jacob fled, and years later, when he returned, they were reconciled. To achieve reconciliation, the proud, ambitious Jacob had to humble himself, and his enemy, Esau, had to forgive him, forgetting the terrible way he had been wronged.

—Douglas Stuart

For Personal Insight and Group Discussion

1. In 1 John 4:19-21, John gives a strong measure by which we can judge our own commitment to God. Under what circumstances have I tried to love God while maintaining unloving attitudes toward others?

2. What excuses have I used to justify holding a grudge against another?

3. What is our motivation for loving, according to 1 John 4:19? Does a person have to be lovable before I can love him?

4. What steps are necessary to achieve reconciliation between estranged members of the body of Christ?

Obedience and Love

"How does one attain to the perfection Jesus demanded? I believe it can be accomplished by looking at God's perfection and the perfect love of Christ, which sought the greatest and highest welfare of everyone by showing forgiveness in action. Christ was calling his followers to unclench their fists and learn the power of love."

—*Helen W. Kooiman*[8]

I will heal their waywardness and love them freely, for my anger has turned away from them. (Hosea 14:4)

Reconciliation to God involves a change of behavior on our part, but it brings the enjoyment of God's love for us. Reconciliation means that the natural consequences of the wrath of God have been removed from our future.

Sinfulness is the root cause of our waywardness. Hosea compares Israel to a wife who is unfaithful to her "husband" (God), always going elsewhere for love. God graciously woos her back and forgives her, but he also causes her to discontinue her waywardness (Hosea 2:2-15). To be reconciled is to be obedient: "He died for all, that those who live should no longer live for themselves but for him who died for them and was raised again" (2 Corinthians 5:15).

God helps the Christian not just to have reconciliation but to live a reconciled life. Our waywardness can be cured. Without God's help no one can live a godly life. But when "all things are new" (cf. 5:17) by God's grace, even those who have previously resisted God's healing of the heart can believe and obey.

With reconciliation also comes God's love. Hosea describes it as a free, voluntary love, not one that is earned. And this love is for the whole world. It was God's love for the whole world that caused him to send his Son to die for all. He chose to do it, even though the world has not as a whole chosen to respond.

For those people who do respond, however, God's anger is gone. Jesus Christ "rescues us from the coming wrath" (1 Thessalonians 1:10) if we trust in him. A judgment is coming for the whole world. Everyone who has ever lived must "appear before the judgment seat of Christ, that each one may receive what is due him" (2 Corinthians 5:10). Those already reconciled, however, do not fear that judgment. God is not our enemy but our friend. Christ is not a hostile judge, but one who loves us and gave his life for us.

—Douglas Stuart

For Personal Insight and Group Discussion

1. Hosea uses marriage as a symbol of Israel's relationship with God. How is my relationship with God like a marriage? (See 2 Corinthians 11:2.)

2. Israel, God's "bride," was unfaithful to him time after time. How am I unfaithful to God and neglectful of his love?

3. In what ways have I tried to live a godly life and failed? Why did I fail?

4. Although I can never earn or deserve God's love, how can I put myself in a position to receive it? (See Psalm 51:17.)

Lesson 5
Repentance—A Change of Heart

Change

"The truly repentant sinner has discovered through the renewing work of the Holy Spirit that all his doing is full of sin. His doing is the source of his wretched emptiness, his dark depression and his self-despising. But now he has come undone. He turns from his sinful doing and trusts in what Christ has done. This is the essence of repentance."

—C. John Miller[9]

For godly sorrow worketh repentance to salvation not to be repented of: but the sorrow of the world worketh death. (2 Corinthians 7:10, KJV)

Repentance is much more than mere sorrow, which may be simply regret or shame. Repentance is, rather, that sorrow which is complemented by a change of mind and purpose leading to a new life. Such repentance is characterized by a complete change in our orientation toward sin. Rather than accepting and living in the things of the old life, we "[obey] from the heart" the doctrine of the gospel and become rebels against sin rather than against God (Matthew 3:2; 1 Peter 4:3; Romans 6:17).

The Corinthians represented the latter, as indicated by their positive response to Paul's censure. No church had caused him more anguish with their factions, contentions, and immorality. On at least two occasions he had written stern letters (1 Corinthians 5:9-11; 2 Corinthians 2:3,4). At least one additional visit had been made, with little result (2 Corinthians 2:1; 12:14). Finally Paul received a positive report from Titus which indicated that they had truly repented. Even though many battles remained, the Corinthians could truly be called God's church in that they recognized their own sinfulness.

God demands authentic repentance. Such does not begin when we merely "turn over a new leaf," make great promises, obey a new law, or enter into some type of "bargain" with God. Rather, it begins when we acknowledge our sinfulness with a deep spiritual conviction which moves us to seek a new life in Christ. There can be no true Christianity without such a beginning; God heard the repentant sinner but rejected the Pharisee (Luke 18:9-14). Many who seem unsavable will be saved, while others who have carefully practiced religion for a lifetime will be lost.

—James F. Breckenridge

For Personal Insight and Group Discussion

1. What is the difference between true repentance and making a resolution to change? What has been the outcome of my "resolutions" in the past?

2. Why is recognition and acknowledgement of sin essential to repentance?

3. Explain the difference between "godly sorrow" and the "sorrow of the world."

4. What experiences of "godly sorrow" have I had in recent months? What was the result of that sorrow?

5. What does it mean to "obey from the heart"? (Romans 6:13) What other kinds of "obedience" can I identify in my own life?

Process

"When faith grows into full assurance so that we are certain beyond a doubt that the blood of Jesus has washed us whiter than snow, it is then that repentance reaches to its greatest height. Repentance grows as faith grows. Do not make any mistake about it; repentance is not a thing of days and weeks, a temporary penance to be got over as fast as possible! No, it is the grace of a lifetime, like faith itself. Repentance is the inseparable companion of faith."

—C. H. Spurgeon

If we confess our sins, he is faithful and just to forgive us our sins, and to cleanse us from all unrighteousness. (1 John 1:9, KJV)

John's assurance of God's continuing forgiveness implies that repentance is to be an ongoing process in our lives.

The fact that sin continues as our lifelong opponent is symptomatic of the progressive nature of redemption. Paul emphasizes this when he reminds us that we have received the "firstfruits of the Spirit," in anticipation of the redemption of our bodies (Romans 8:18-25, KJV).

The reality of continual warfare with sin creates two dissenting groups. The first are those who see the gospel as a new law. They know all too well they they could never satisfy the law of God. They simply say, "I can't live like that," and reject Christ outright. Others accept Christ but face continual frustration in their failure to conquer sin.

Both groups must be reminded that God is not an adversary to his children. Those who believe are "dead to sin" and their life is "hid with Christ in God." Christians experience "no condemnation" before God. The fact that we are not perfect only serves to remind us further of our reliance upon continuing grace from God. Thus, the law that cannot save us also cannot condemn us either (Colossians 3:3; Romans 8:1, KJV).

The life of true repentance shows a newness, not in perfection but in motivation. Luther faced a great dilemma after he had found the truth of justification by faith only to realize that he was still a sinner. His solution was not to deny the existence of sin, but rather to affirm the total grace of God in viewing us as already forgiven through Christ. The mark of the Christian is not the absence of sin but rather our constant confession and dependence upon God and his righteousness.

—James F. Breckenridge

For Personal Insight and Group Discussion

1. If Christ died once for the forgiveness of my sin, why do I need to repent more than once?

2. Why do I often resist repenting, even when I know I have sinned?

3. What are the results of repentance in my relationship with God? In my relationships with others? (See 1 John 1:7.)

4. What is the difference between feeling convicted of sin and feeling condemned? How can I recognize and repent of sin and still experience freedom from condemnation? (See Romans 8:1-17.)

Lesson 6
Repentance—A Change of Habit

Progress

"Too easily we equate repentance with being sorry. But being sorry is only part of it. We haven't repented until our sorrow causes a change of mind about our sin, and that results in a change of attitude. When God shows us that our speech, attitude or action is wrong, then we repent and change direction to go his way."

—*Marian Jones Clark[10]*

Therefore bring forth fruit in keeping with repentance. (Matthew 3:8, NASB)

Multitudes came to John the Baptist to acknowledge their sins and be baptized as a symbol of their new spiritual understanding. Also present were the Pharisees and Sadducees. The former were moral rigorists who doted on legalistic interpretations of the Law. The latter were the priestly "liberals" who compromised with everyone and everything. Both groups received the same message: "Prove your repentance by the fruit it bears" (Matthew 3:8, NEB).

John comes to us with the same message. Some of us, like the Pharisees, have overemphasized the externals of religion. We fail to see that spirituality is always measured by the inward qualities which define the devoted life (Galatians 5:22,23). Others, like the Sadducees, have sought compromise with the world. We need to be reminded that God calls us to a true and biblical holiness.

The effect of true repentance is a life which shows constant progress and growth congruent with a new life (Hebrews 6:1). Particularly instructive is Paul's admonition to the Philippians: "Work out your salvation with fear and trembling." We have the substance of salvation, grace in Jesus Christ, but it is our responsibility to build upon it in a manner which shows spiritual growth and consistency (Philippians 2:12; Ephesians 1:13).

The Bible simply does not address the possibility that one might be a child of God and not bear spiritual fruit (Matthew 7:17,18). The book of Hebrews continually warns that the only true test of the Christian life is the Christian life (Hebrews 3:6,14; 10:23,24,39; 12:28).

Even the apostle Paul did not take his spirituality for granted and daily sought victory over the flesh. Any self-indulgence or conformity to the world meant spiritual peril. He commanded that we are not to take part in even the slightest form of sin; instead, we are to realize a growth from experience to maturity in a life which is constantly moving from faith into greater faith (1 Corinthians 9:24,27;10:22; 1 Thessalonians 5:22; Romans 1:17;5:3-5).

—James F. Breckenridge

For Personal Insight and Group Discussion

1. If we are saved by grace through faith, what does Paul mean by his instructions in Philippians 2, "Work out your salvation in fear and trembling"?

2. What does John mean when he calls the Pharisees to produce the "fruit of repentance"?

3. What "fruit of repentance" might be appropriate in my life?

4. In what specific ways can I respond to God's call for repentance by a change of behavior?

Restitution

*"Repentance is re-entry into communion. It is reconciliation of those
who have fallen out, a justification of the fellow man, a sanctification
of the soul and the person. Repentance is the stirring of a new life in
fellow men "dead in sin," and with it the emergence of a new mind."*

—*Joseph Haroutunian[11]*

And Zacchaeus stood, and said unto the Lord; Behold, Lord, the
half of my goods I give to the poor; and if I have taken any thing
from any man by false accusation, I restore him fourfold. (Luke
19:8, KJV)

Zacchaeus demonstrates that repentance must be horizontal as
well as vertical. He was a tax collector who assisted in gathering
revenues for Rome. Since great gains could be made from over-
charging, abuses were frequent and Jews classed such officials
as sinners, comparable to harlots and heathens (Matthew 9:11;
18:17;21:31).

Zacchaeus' offer of fourfold restitution represents a heartfelt
faith which complied with the instructions of Moses (Exodus 22:1).
His compliance was complemented by his additional desire to give
half of his goods to the poor. He realized his faith was useless without
practical steps to restore what he had taken from those he may have
wronged.

The truly repentant life will always reflect an attitude of reconciliation. Christ instructed offenders to leave their gift at the altar and
first be "reconciled" to their brother (Matthew 5:22,23). The word
"reconciled" literally means to change our feelings toward others in
such a manner that their feelings will change toward us. We must
demonstrate a willingness to settle all accounts.

Christ demands that we make restitution to people we have
wronged. This may seem impossible at first, especially when hurts

have continued for years and relationships seem permanently altered. Yet the same Spirit who gives peace with God will also give us peace with each other. The Bible promises that a strength greater than ours will be provided (Isaiah 41:10).

Christianity cannot be a private affair. True repentance brings a changed attitude to the sphere of human relations.

—James F. Breckenridge

For Personal Insight and Group Discussion

1. Under what circumstances does repentance call for restitution?

2. What kinds of restitution might be in order? Give several examples.

3. What particular situations in my life need repentance? What situations call for reconciliation or restitution?

4. What specific steps can I take to demonstrate "horizontal repentance"—the willingness to make restitution to those I have wronged?

Lesson 7
Fellowship—The Inward Bond

Oneness

"A habit of devout fellowship with God is the spring of all our life, and the strength of it."

—*H. E. Manning*[12]

They devoted themselves to the apostles' teaching and to the fellowship, to the breaking of bread and to prayer. (Acts 2:42)

This summary verse describes what was important for maintaining the life of a Christian in the early church. Fellowship is among the basics—and fellowship is no mere social gathering. Christian fellowship meant that believers were held together in Christ. Wherever they went, whatever they did, the Christians were one in spirit.

The redwoods of California reach upward to great heights—some more than three hundred feet—and they have weathered the storms of centuries. The strength of the redwoods is in their roots. The roots of one tree intertwine with the roots of others, and they literally hold each other up. Similarly, in the fellowship of Christians, our strength and our fruits grow from a unity with Christ and a oneness with each other (John 15:5-8; 1 Corinthians 12:12,13).

"Koinonia," the Greek word for fellowship, has various shades of meaning, including "close relationship." For the Christian this includes a new relationship established between the believer and Christ. "God is faithful, by whom you were called into the fellowship of his Son, Jesus Christ our Lord" (1 Corinthians 1:9,RSV).

Another mark of Christian fellowship is one's association with the Holy Spirit and with other believers. The early Christians were together and had everything in common. "They broke bread in their homes and ate together with glad and sincere hearts, praising God and enjoying the favor of all the people" (Acts 2:44,46,47).

—*Lewis Foster*

For Personal Insight and Group Discussion

1. What is true fellowship? How, and under what circumstances, have I experienced true fellowship?

2. How does fellowship help me gain stability in my Christian life?

3. In John 17:20,21, Jesus prayed that his disciples would become one. In practical terms, what does that oneness mean?

4. Philippians 2:2 encourages us to "have the same mind" with one another and with Christ. How, with our varieties of ideas and opinions, can Christians share "one mind"?

Participation

"Fellowship is heaven, and lack of fellowship is hell; fellowship is life, and lack of fellowship is death; and the deeds that ye do upon the earth, it is for fellowship's sake that ye do them."

—*William Morris*

I thank my God upon every remembrance of you, . . . for your fellowship in the gospel from the first day until now. (Philippians 1:3,5, NKJV)

Christian fellowship expressed by the term "koinonia" does not denote a spectator role among the Christians. It means "participation." The Christian has a "partnership in the gospel" (Philippians 1:5). When a Christian worships, he is not a spectator, he is a participant. When a Christian witnesses concerning his hope in Christ, or when he makes his contributions in the name of Christ, he is not a spectator, but a participant.

Paul described the Lord's Supper to the Corinthians as a time of participation: "Is not the cup of thanksgiving for which we give thanks a participation [koinonia] in the blood of Christ? And is not the bread that we break a participation [koinonia] in the body of Christ? Because there is one loaf, we, who are many, are one body, for we all partake of the one loaf" (1 Corinthians 10:16,17). The Christian has fellowship (communion) with God, in Christ, and with fellow Christians. In this he has a fellowship of oneness, a fellowship of joy the world cannot know, a fellowship of partners in commitment.

The apostle John testified, "We proclaim to you what we have seen and heard, so that you also may have fellowship with us. And our fellowship is with the Father and with his Son, Jesus Christ. We write this to make our joy complete" (1 John 1:3,4). Christians participate in rich fruits of fellowship.

—*Lewis Foster*

For Personal Insight and Group Discussion

1. What does being a "partner in the gospel" mean?

2. How is my "partnership" expressed in my participation in Christian fellowship?

3. In 1 Corinthians 12, Paul describes the church as a "body." How do the members of my physical body work together?

4. What function do I contribute to the smooth working of the spiritual body?

5. Why is fellowship with one another essential to the Christian life?

Lesson 8
Fellowship—The Outward Sign

Sharing

"Christians may not see eye to eye, but they can walk arm in arm."

—Brotherhood Journal[13]

I pray that the fellowship of your faith may become effective through the knowledge of every good thing which is in you for Christ's sake. (Philemon 6, NASB)

Just as it is impossible to love without giving, so it is impossible to have fellowship without "sharing" (Philemon 6). This is another side to koinonia. The Christian message added a dimension to this meaning that the secular world seldom glimpsed.

Paul asked Philemon to share (koinonia) his faith. This meant that he must receive Onesimus, the runaway slave, as a brother. He must live out the gospel. In Hebrews we read, "And do not forget to do good and to share [koinonia] with others, for with such sacrifices God is pleased" (Hebrews 13:16).

When Paul wrote of making "a contribution for the poor among the saints in Jerusalem" (Romans 15:26), he used the word koinonia, an offering, a sharing. This is the same offering he was speaking of when he described the giving of the Macedonians: "Entirely on their own, they urgently pleaded with us for the privilege of sharing [koinonia] in this service to the saints. And they did not do as we expected, but they gave themselves first to the Lord and then to us in keeping with God's will" (2 Corinthians 8:3-5).

In the Jerusalem church, sharing was carried to an extent reflected nowhere else in the early church. Some sold their property and gave the proceeds to the church. They had all things in common. The Christians not only shared their possessions, but they shared the very experiences of Christ. The Christians were even willing to share Paul's suffering (Acts 4:32). Such sharing is evidence of true fellowship.

—Lewis Foster

For Personal Insight and Group Discussion

1. What kind of commitment is essential to true fellowship?

2. How can my commitment to others be demonstrated in practical ways?

3. In Colossians 3:12-17, Paul gives some practical advice on living in fellowship with one another. In what specific ways, or in what relationships, can I begin to:

    a) clothe myself with compassion?

    b) bear with others, and forgive?

    c) let the peace of Christ rule in my heart?

    d) let the word of Christ dwell in me?

    e) teach and admonish others?

Living

"Jesus throws down the dividing prejudices of nationality, and teaches universal love, without distinction of race, merit, or rank—a man's neighbor is everyone that needs help."

—John Cunningham Geikie[14]

If we walk in the light, as he is in the light, we have fellowship with one another, and the blood of Jesus, his Son, purifies us from every sin. (1 John 1:7)

To put our lives in the hand of God means that we must turn our backs on Satan (James 4:4-7). To be in fellowship with God means that we must break fellowship with the world. Where our fellowship is becomes proof of where our hearts are.

To think we can maintain a supportive relationship with unbelief is wrong. Those who deny the Scriptures and place man's authority above God's Word cannot claim to be his followers. "Do not be yoked together with unbelievers. For what do righteousness and wickedness have in common? Or what fellowship can light have with darkness?" (2 Corinthians 6:14) Fellowship is broken when false doctrine divides us from God's Word, or false living divides us from God's ways, or hypocrisy places barriers of separation between us and God or his people (2 John 9-11; 1 Corinthians 5:11-13; 1 John 1:6,7).

When Adam sinned, fellowship with God was broken. All of us have sinned and are separated from our Creator. But God made possible a reconciliation through his own Son. Now we can have fellowship with God. Our fellowship with others in the faith is a mark of our reconciliation to God.

—Lewis Foster

For Personal Insight and Group Discussion

1. What does Paul mean in 2 Corinthians 6:14 when he warns Christians not to be "unequally yoked" with unbelievers? Does Paul mean that I am not to associate with non-Christians?

2. What is the difference between rejecting Satan and the world's value system, and rejecting lost people for whom Christ died?

3. How can I maintain the "yoke of fellowship" with believers and still cultivate relationships with unbelievers?

4. In what specific ways have I broken fellowship with the world in turning to Christ? What other areas of "worldly fellowship" need to be broken in my life?

5. How can I communicate love and acceptance to those who don't know Christ without seeming to condone their sinful lifestyles?

Lesson 9
Mercy—God Reaches

God, Our Creator and Redeemer

"Only the mercy of God's grace saves us from our having to pay the wages of sin."

—*Walter H. Brovald*[15]

The Lord is gracious and compassionate, slow to anger and rich in love. The Lord is good to all; he has compassion on all he has made. (Psalm 145:8,9)

In the Bible the word "mercy" is used to express kindness shown in situations of distress and suffering. The merciful person is someone who reaches out in compassion to others, especially those who are helpless.

The Bible emphasizes that mercy begins with God. God is our merciful Creator. In his kindness God made us in his image, so that we may fellowship with him and enjoy the rest of creation.

Even when mankind spurned his kindness and fell into sin, God did not turn his back, but remained faithful to his handiwork. Despite our rebellion, "he is kind to the ungrateful and wicked" (Luke 6:35). He delays the final judgment on unrepentant sinners, and in his mercy God offers salvation to sinners. Mercy is God "looking down upon man in his pitiful condition as the result of sin, and having pity upon him."[16] God not only alleviates human misery but deals with the source of that misery—sin.

Because of his mercy, God sent his only Son into the world to do for us what we are unable to do for ourselves (Luke 1:68-79). The sacrificial death of Christ not only displays the justice of God—his wrath and curse on sin—but it also reveals the depths of his love and saving compassion. The supreme example of mercy is the cross of Jesus Christ.

—*Richard B. Gaffin, Jr.*

For Personal Insight and Group Discussion

1. What does "mercy" mean? How does God show "mercy" in dealing with his people?

2. How does an understanding of God's mercy affect the way I respond to others?

3. What are some specific ways I have seen God's mercy demonstrated in my life?

Christ, Our High Priest

"The centrality of our Christian faith is the love of God exhibited on the cross of Calvary—an unconditional love totally unmerited. How remarkable and reassuring that nothing can wedge itself between the love of God and the saint."

—*Jean Dusting*[17]

Let us then approach the throne of grace with confidence, so that we may receive mercy and find grace to help us in our time of need. (Hebrews 4:16)

Christ is our merciful High Priest because of what he has already done for his people. Like the Old Testament priests, Jesus sacrificed to God, but unlike them, he offered himself. The blood that he shed was not that of goats and bulls, but his very own lifeblood. Also, unlike the Old Testament priests, he did not have to offer sacrifices for his own sins, because he was "holy, blameless, [and] pure" (Hebrews 7:26).

Christ's self-sacrifice has reconciled us to God. It has turned aside God's wrath and removed the alienation between him and ourselves caused by sin. The one sacrifice of Christ accomplished this "once for all" (Hebrews 7:27).

Jesus is a merciful High Priest because of what he continues to do for his people. Christ is in heaven "now to appear for us in God's presence." He is the living seal and exhibition of our righteousness. He prays for his people: "He always lives to intercede for them" (Hebrews 9:24;7:25).

Jesus prays for us because the devil is prowling around like a roaring lion seeking to devour us. He prays for us, as he did for Peter, that our faith will not fail. He prays for us because he knows our weaknesses and temptations. He experienced those temptations when he was on earth; yet he overcame them and so "he is able to help those who are being tempted" (1 Peter 5:8; Luke 22:31,32; Hebrews 2:18).

Our confidence in prayer lies not in ourselves but in our High Priest who prays for us. Because Christ is praying for his church, we know that we can approach God; we can come to "the throne of grace" (Hebrews 4:16). And because our High Priest is praying for us today, we can be sure that the mercy we receive will be timely—it will come when we need it.

—Richard B. Gaffin, Jr.

For Personal Insight and Group Discussion

1. Hebrews 4:14-5:10 and 7:23-28 describe Jesus as a high priest like the priests of the Old Testament. What are some of the similarities between Christ's priesthood and the priests of the Old Testament?

2. What are some significant differences?

3. Why is it important that Jesus died "once for all when he offered himself" (Hebrews 7:27)? What does the verse mean to me in terms of my forgiveness?

4. Why is it important that Jesus was tempted just as I am?

5. Why is it important to me that he prays for me before the Father?

Lesson 10
Mercy—Our Response

Imitating God, Our Great Example

"When we are battered by life, we want a merciful God to pick us up from the roadside and carry us to an inn. We want our hunger and thirst quenched, our wounds bound and a comfortable place to recuperate from the blows of the wicked. Can we give less and call it mercy? Mercy is more than casual kindness. Mercy demands commitment."

—*Madonna Yates*[18]

Be merciful, just as your Father is merciful. (Luke 6:36)

The model for Christian discipleship is God himself. The New Testament calls believers to "imitate" Christ and to be conformed to his "image" (Romans 8:29; 1 Corinthians 11:1,2; 2 Corinthians 3:18; Ephesians 5:1).

The principle of imitation finds its ultimate expression in Jesus' statement in the Sermon on the Mount: "Be perfect, therefore, as your heavenly Father is perfect." The principle is that Christians are to love as God loves, not only some people but all people, our enemies as well as our friends and neighbors (Matthew 5:43-48). "Mercy" refers to loving compassion that reaches out to all, unreservedly and without bias, to friend and foe alike. Everything Christians think and do ought to be patterned after God, but nowhere is that imitation more apparent than in showing total and uninhibited mercy.

The model for mercy is God, as our Father. We are to be kind and loving to all because we are "sons of the Most High" (Luke 6:35). On our own we would never imitate God, but God has had compassion on us—he has broken that power of sin in our lives. In doing so he has also adopted us into his family. This means that in the church, "God's household" (1 Timothy 3:15), we ought to see a family resemblance between the Father and his children.

Christian compassion reaches out to alleviate suffering and

misery, but such compassion also addresses the ultimate source of all human misery—sin and rebellion against God. Christian mercy knows no conflict between evangelism and social action.

—Richard B. Gaffin, Jr.

For Personal Insight and Group Discussion

1. What does it mean to "imitate Christ"? What do Christ's life and character demonstrate about mercy?

2. Luke 10:25-37 presents a striking example of mercy. What are some of the qualities in the Samaritan that demonstrate mercy?

3. How can I begin to be more aware of God's mercy in my own life?

4. What steps can I take to extend that mercy to others?

5. What particular people in my life need to see God's mercy demonstrated through me? How can I begin to relate to them in a Christlike way?

Forgiving Others, Our Great Privilege

"The eyes of mercy are deep with compassionate glances, full of tears, the homes of prayer; the feet of mercy are soft in their tread, for they will not break the bruised reed nor quench the smoldering spark in the dimly burning flax; the voice of mercy is generous to the fallen, gentle to the weak and gracious to the offender; from the heart of mercy soothing balm flows to the wounds of sinners, of sufferers and of the world."

—F.B. Meyer[19]

Be kind and compassionate to one another, forgiving each other, just as in Christ God forgave you. (Ephesians 4:32)

Just as our heavenly Father freely forgives us of our sins, so for us, his children, no expression of mercy is more essential than freely forgiving others.

In the Lord's Prayer Jesus teaches us to pray: "Forgive us our debts, as we also have forgiven our debtors." He goes on, "For if you forgive men when they sin against you, your heavenly Father will also forgive you. But if you do not forgive men their sins, your Father will not forgive your sins" (Matthew 6:12,14,15). And in the fifth Beatitude Jesus, no doubt with forgiveness in mind, said, "Blessed are the merciful, for they will be shown mercy" (Matthew 5:7).

Is Jesus intending to say that we will be forgiven and receive mercy on the basis of our record of forgiving others? Hardly; if that were the case, no one would have any hope of forgiveness.

But Jesus does intend to teach us that there is an intrinsic connection between our being forgiven by God and our readiness to forgive others. The sole condition for forgiveness is repentance.

Repentance includes the recognition that we can make no claim on God except to claim his gracious promise to forgive. Thus we are bound to be merciful and forgiving to others. A readiness to forgive shows that we have grasped the reality of our own forgiveness. That readiness is not merely a "good intention"; it persists toward concrete acts of forgiveness and the desire for reconciliation.

The Bible's teaching on mercy may be summed up this way: The supreme expression of mercy is God's forgiving us, and one of our greatest privileges is to forgive others.

—Richard B. Gaffin, Jr.

For Personal Insight and Group Discussion

1. God offers us forgiveness out of his grace and mercy, not because of anything we do to deserve it. Yet the Lord's Prayer teaches us to pray, "forgive us as we forgive others." How does our forgiveness of others affect our experience of God's forgiveness?

2. Does my forgiveness of someone who has wronged me depend upon that person's confession and repentance? Why or why not? How might this insight affect some specific relationship in my life?

3. When reconciliation, the ultimate goal of forgiveness, is impossible, how can I live at peace and enjoy the fruit of God's forgiveness?

Lesson 11
Love—God's Initiative

Electing Love

"I think that love is the only spiritual power that can overcome the self-centeredness that is inherent in being alive. Love is the thing that makes life possible or, indeed, tolerable."

—Arnold Toynbee

I have loved you with an everlasting love; therefore I have continued my faithfulness to you. (Jeremiah 31:3, RSV)

The word for love used in the Old Testament incorporates a variety of meanings. Unlike the Greek language of the New Testament, the Hebrew language utilizes only one word for all expressions of love. Love is the opposite of hate (Malachi 1:2,3), and implies that one yearns to be near the beloved. One who loves deeply desires to be united with another in affection and in life's relationships. Love not only describes an inner preference for someone, it also includes a conscious act on behalf of the beloved. Love wishes to choose or elect one to whom affection can be given.

God chose Israel as a special people to enjoy divine favor (Deuteronomy 4:37). Deuteronomy and the prophetic books reminded Israel of the distinctiveness of her relationship with God. God's love did not change when his people were unfaithful. Rather, God attempted to draw Israel back to himself. The prophet Hosea especially grasped this truth because of his rejection by an unfaithful wife. For unfaithful lovers, the way back to a renewed relationship, he said, comes primarily through God's patient, faithful love (Hosea 2:14,15;11:4).

Hosea's experience with Gomer paints a graphic picture of God's faithfulness to us. Even when we have been unfaithful, God continues to love us with the same faithfulness. Everlasting love always reaches out to even the unfaithful. Forgiveness draws all to salvation who accept God's love in truth and fidelity.

—J. Gordon Harris

For Personal Insight and Group Discussion

1. How do I know when I love someone? Are those characteristics true of God's love for me? (See Matthew 23:37.)

2. Why does God love me? How do I know he loves me? (See 1 John 4:7-9.)

3. What does 2 Timothy 2:13 indicate about the constancy of God's love? Why is he ever faithful to me?

4. How do I respond to a beloved one who betrays me? How does God respond to my faithlessness to him? (See 2 Timothy 2:13.)

Reflected Love

"It is not a question of how much we know, how clever we are, nor even how good; it all depends upon the heart's love. External actions are the results of love, the fruit it bears; but the source, the root, is in the deep of the heart."

—*Francois Fenelon*

You shall love the Lord your God with all your heart, and with all your soul, and with all your might (Deuteronomy 6:5, RSV). You shall love your neighbor as yourself (Leviticus 19:18, RSV). The stranger who sojourns with you . . . you shall love him as yourself. (Leviticus 19:34, RSV)

As God reaches out in love with complete devotion, so God's people are to return this affection in the same spirit. Believers reflect this love in their relationships both with God and with other persons. This response summarizes the heart of God's commandments in both the Old and New Testaments (Mark 12:30,31):

(1) *Love God totally.* Believers have been called in the Bible to respond with total devotion to God's love and grace. Jesus likewise teaches that the total effort of a believer needs to be concentrated on loving him. Love for God indicates that the loyalties and worship of the faithful focus first on the divine will. Loving believers express their devotion to God in service (Matthew 10:37,38; Deuteronomy 10:12;11:13,22).

(2) *Love others selflessly.* God's love not only demands total devotion in worship and service, it stretches believers to consider the needs of others. People tend to limit their love to those with whom they feel comfortable. The struggle to feel responsible for "outsiders" dominates the book of Jonah and the question of the lawyer to Jesus: "Who is my neighbor?" (Luke 10:29, RSV) Jesus' parable of the Good Samaritan extends the horizons of love to

include the needs of strangers (Leviticus 19:34). Helping them is to assume the same priority as taking care of personal needs. Such concern encompasses the nature and scope of reflected divine love.

—*J. Gordon Harris*

For Personal Insight and Group Discussion

1. Are the characteristics I associate with love present in my relationship with God? What emotions and thoughts, specifically, characterize my love for the Lord?

2. How does my awareness of God's love for me enhance my love for others?

3. What changes do I need to make in my life and attitudes in order to focus on:

   a) loving God totally?

   b) loving others selflessly?

Lesson 12
Love—Our Response

Shared Love

"The churches would soon be filled if outsiders could find that people in them loved them when they came. This love draws sinners! We must win them to us first, then we can win them to Christ. We must get people to love us, and then turn them over to Christ."

—*D. L. Moody*

Dear friends, let us love one another, for love comes from God. Everyone who loves has been born of God and knows God. Whoever does not love does not know God, because God is love. (1 John 4:7,8)

Divine love characterizes the children of God in the letters of John. Christian love depends on God for its definition and origin. As Paul teaches, love is the greatest of all Christian evidences (1 Corinthians 13:13):

(1) *Sharing love establishes community.* Loving one another demonstrates that we live in the Light. Lovelessness, on the other hand, shows that darkness and blindness dominate our sinful existence. Fellowship with God expresses itself in fellowship with one another (1 John 2:9-11). Shared love does not stir up strife but enables believers to love one another despite the hurt of offenses.

(2) *Sharing love expresses God's salvation.* With many popular, cheap imitations of love available, it is important that Christians love with a depth and breadth made possible only by knowing God. Shared love, which Christians are challenged to show, should flow out of the "newness" of life when one is "born of God." The new birth initiates a fresh ability to love. God's salvation remains absolutely necessary before persons can love in the fullness of Christ (1 John 4:13-16).

Sharing love should develop out of a growing relationship with

Christ. To know God is to become close and intimate friends with him, and out of this growing intimacy comes an ability to love (1 John 4:16-18).

—*J. Gordon Harris*

For Personal Insight and Group Discussion

1. What "imitations" of love are evident in the world around me?

2. Is the church prone to "imitation love" as well? Give examples.

3. How did Christ express true love to those who followed him? Did his love always "look" loving?

4. How, specifically, can I demonstrate real love in my own fellowship?

Redeeming Love

"You called, you cried, you shattered my deafness, you sparkled, you blazed, you drove away my blindness, you shed your fragrance, and I drew in my breath, and I pant for you."

—*Saint Augustine*

For God so loved the world that he gave his only Son, that whoever believes in him shall not perish but have eternal life. (John 3:16)

At the cross Jesus demonstrated that God's redeeming love knows no limits. God loved a lost world so much that no sacrifice was too great—Jesus relinquished glory to suffer humiliation as a crucified servant (Philippians 2:5-8). Redemption brought the love of God clearly into focus, and redeeming love was the motivation for God's effort to provide hope for a dying world. Love motivated Jesus to become the ultimate sacrifice for sin. Compassion moved the Ruler of the universe to sacrifice his Son, his most precious possession. By this act, godly love stands defined as self-giving rather than self-serving (1 Corinthians 13:5).

God's act of self-giving provides the way of salvation for everyone. The promise of salvation to "whoever believes" offers hope to all individuals. Redeeming love never feels content while some still perish (Ezekiel 18:32).

Eternal life for believers remains the premier gift of redeeming love. It opens, for all who accept it, a life in God's love and in loving one another.

—*J. Gordon Harris*

For Personal Insight and Group Discussion

1. Has my love most often been self-giving or self-serving? Give examples.

2. Christ redeemed the world through loving sacrifice. How can I, as a member of his body, lay down my life for others?

3. 1 Corinthians 13 is an eloquent biblical definition of love. How can I apply each of the characteristics of love listed in that chapter to my own life in Christ, and to my relationships with others?

Notes

[1] Quoted in *Decision* (October, 1985), 35.

[2] Oswald Chambers, *The Place of Help* (Dodd, Mead & Co., 1936), 218.

[3] Erwin W. Lutzer, *How to Say No to a Stubborn Habit* (Wheaton, Illinois: SP Publications, Victor Books, 1979), 89.

[4] A. W. Tozer, *That Incredible Christian* (Camp Hill, Pennsylvania: Christian Publications, 1964), 45,46.

[5] Charles Colson, *Who Speaks for God?* (Westchester, Illinois: Good News/Crossway Books, 1985), 78.

[6] Quoted in *Decision* (June, 1986), 35.

[7] Marion Leach Jacobsen, *Saints and Snobs* (Wheaton, Illinois: Tyndale House, 1972), 167.

[8] Helen W. Kooiman, *Forgiveness in Action* (New York: E. Dutton, 1974), 129,130.

[9] C. John Miller, *Repentance and 20th Century Man* (Fort Washington, Pennsylvania: Christian Literature Crusade, 1980), 23.

[10] Quoted in *Decision* (July/August, 1986), 35.

[11] Joseph Haroutunian, "A Theology of Repentance," in *Christianity and World Revolution*, Edwin H. Rian, ed., (San Francisco: Harper and Row, 1963), 216.

[12] Quoted in George Sweeting, *Great Quotes and Illustrations* (Waco, Texas: Word, 1985), 116.

[13] Quoted in Frank S. Mead, *Encyclopedia of Religious Quotations* (Old Tappan, New Jersey: Fleming H. Revell, 1965), 37.

[14] Ibid., 38.

[15] Walter H. Brovald, *Meditations on Matthew* (St. Paul, Minnesota: Gryphon Press, 1977), 33.

[16] D. Martyn Lloyd-Jones, *Studies in the Sermon on the Mount, Vol. I* (Grand Rapids, Michigan: Wm. B. Eerdmans, 1959), 100.

[17] Quoted in *Decision* (October, 1986), 35.

[18] Ibid.

[19] F. B. Meyer, *Inherit the Kingdom: Meditations of the Sermon on the Mount* (Wheaton, Illinois: SP Publications, Victor Books), 25.

About the Authors

John F. Walvoord

has been a faculty member at Dallas Theological Seminary for fifty years and now serves as the seminary's chancellor.

Douglas Stuart, Ph.D.,

is a professor of Old Testament at Gordon-Conwell Theological Seminary in South Hamilton, Massachusetts, and the author of several books, including *Favorite Old Testament Passages* and *Old Testament Exegesis.*

James F. Breckenridge

is professor of theology at East Coast Bible College in Charlotte, North Carolina. He is the author of several articles and a book, *The Theological Self-Understanding of the Catholic Charismatic Movement.*

Lewis Foster, Ph.D.,

is professor of New Testament at Cincinnati Christian Seminary in Cincinnati, Ohio. He is the author of numerous articles and books, including *Selecting a Translation of the Bible* and *The Only Way.*

Richard B. Gaffin, Jr., Th.D.,

is professor of systematic theology at Westminster Theological Seminary in Philadelphia, Pennsylvania. He is the author of *Perspectives on Pentecost* and editor of *Redemptive History and Biblical Interpretation: The Shorter Writings of Geerhardus Vos.*

J. Gordon Harris, Ph.D.

is vice president for academic affairs and professor of Old Testament at North American Baptist Seminary, Sioux Falls, South Dakota. He is the author of numerous articles and books, including *Biblical Perspectives on Aging.*